Riddledy Piggledy

I'm Mother Goose. Come, take a look.
I've put together a riddle book.
Read out each rhyme and guess the song
where all the riddledy things belong.

Riddledy Piggledy

Tony Mitton

Illustrated by
Paddy Mounter

PICTURE CORGI

RIDDLEDY PIGGLEDY
A PICTURE CORGI BOOK 0 552 54819 7

First published in Great Britain by David Fickling Books
an imprint of Random House Children's Books

David Fickling Books edition published 2004
Picture Corgi edition published 2005

1 3 5 7 9 10 8 6 4 2

Text copyright © Tony Mitton, 2004
Illustrations copyright © Paddy Mounter, 2004

The right of Tony Mitton to be identified as the author and Paddy Mounter
to be identified as the illustrator of this work has been asserted in
accordance with the Copyright, Designs and Patents Act 1988.

Picture Corgi Books are published by Random House Children's Books,
61–63 Uxbridge Road, London W5 58A
a division of The Random House Group Ltd,
in Australia by Random House Australia (Pty) Ltd,
20 Alfred Street, Milsons Point, Sydney, NSW 2061, Australia
in New Zealand by Random House New Zealand Ltd,
18 Poland Road, Glenfield, Auckland 10, New Zealand,
and in South Africa by Random House (Pty) Ltd,
Endulini, 5A Jubilee Road, Parktown 2193, South Africa

THE RANDOM HOUSE GROUP Limited Reg. No. 954009
www.kidsatrandomhouse.co.uk

A CIP catalogue record for this book is available from the British Library.

Printed in Malaysia

Contents

To Mum, with love.
TM*x*

Soggy Boggy Bag

A doctor's bag
in a bit of a muddle
dropped beside a very deep puddle,
lost in Gloucester in a shower of rain
(but nobody came back
to get it again).

What's the answer? Let me see · · ·
Have a think. Now, what can it be · · ?

Doctor Foster

Doctor Foster went to Gloucester
in a shower of rain.
He stepped in a puddle
right up to his middle
and never went there again.

Quick Cake

A cake marked B
that still feels hot.
Someone must be
missing it a lot.

What's the answer? Let me see · · ·
Have a think. Now, what can it be · · ?

Pat-a-Cake, Pat-a-Cake

Pat-a-cake, pat-a-cake, baker's man,
bake me a cake as fast as you can.
Pat it and prick it and mark it with B
and put it in the oven
for Baby and me.

Sky Pie

Some bread and honey
and an empty pie,
and a bunch of blackbirds
singing nearby.

What's the answer? Let me see · · ·
Have a think. Now, what can it be · · ?

Sing a Song of Sixpence

Sing a song of sixpence, a pocket full of rye.
Four and twenty blackbirds baked in a pie.
When the pie was opened the birds began to sing.
Wasn't that a dainty dish to set before the king?

The king was in his counting-house,
counting out his money.
The queen was in the parlour,
eating bread and honey.
The maid was in the garden,
hanging out the clothes,
when down came a blackbird
and pecked off her nose.

Cobble Cottage

A great big shoe the size of a house
that makes a man seem small as a mouse.
There's a door in the heel,
and windows too.
Somebody lives here!
I wonder who?

What's the answer? Let me see · · ·
Have a think. Now, what can it be · · ·?

There was an Old Woman who Lived in a Shoe

There was an old woman who lived in a shoe.
She had so many children,
she didn't know what to do.
She gave them some broth with plenty of bread,
then kissed them all sweetly
and tucked them in bed.

Sneeze-Up

Lots of roses arranged in a ring.
And a box of tissues –
what a strange thing!

What's the answer? Let me see · · ·
Have a think. Now, what can it be · · ?

Ring-a-Ring o' Roses

Ring-a-ring o' roses,
a pocket full of posies.
A-tishoo! A-tishoo!
We all fall down.

Moon Toon

A funny little fiddle
that's out of tune,
found by the light
of the silvery moon
(and some way off:
a dish and a spoon).

What's the answer? Let me see · · ·
Have a think. Now, what can it be · · · ?

Hey Diddle Diddle

Hey diddle diddle,
the cat and the fiddle,
the cow jumped over the moon.
The little dog laughed to see such fun
and the dish ran away
with the spoon.

Splash Crash

A dented bucket
not far from a well.
Maybe somebody
slipped and fell...
(who can tell?)

What's the answer? Let me see · · ·
Have a think. Now, what can it be · · · ?

Jack and Jill

Jack and Jill went up the hill
to fetch a pail of water.
Jack fell down
and broke his crown
and Jill came tumbling after.

Tub Trio

A loaf of bread
(still good to eat)
and a butcher's knife
(for cutting meat)
and a candle-stick
(not quite complete).

What's the answer? Let me see · · ·
Have a think. Now, what can it be · · ?

Rub-a-Dub-Dub

Rub-a-dub-dub, three men in a tub,
and how do you think they got there?
The butcher, the baker, the candlestick-maker,
they all jumped out of a rotten p'tater.
'Twas enough to make a man stare.

Picnic Website

A bowl and a spoon
(with cobwebs on),
but nobody knows
where the owner's gone.

What's the answer? Let me see · · ·
Have a think. Now, what can it be · · ?

Little Miss Muffet

Little Miss Muffet
sat on a tuffet,
eating her curds and whey.
Along came a spider
who sat down beside her
and frightened
Miss Muffet away.

Table for Two

A table for two with the diners gone,
and none of the dishes have anything on.
Maybe they were hungry,
or greedy, or neat,
as they've just left dishes,
but nothing to eat.

What's the answer? Let me see · · ·
Have a think. Now, what can it be · · ?

Jack Sprat

Jack Sprat could eat no fat.
His wife could eat no lean.
And so between the two of them,
they licked the platter clean.

Baabershop

Three bags of wool
(all full),
and in each sack
the wool
is black.

What's the answer? Let me see · · ·
Have a think. Now, what can it be · · ?

Baa Baa, Black Sheep

Baa baa, black sheep,
have you any wool?
Yes sir, yes sir,
three bags full.
One for the master
and one for the dame.
And one for the little boy
who lives down the lane.

Good Plum Pud

A Christmas pie
with a hole in the lid.
I didn't do it.
I wonder who did?

What's the answer? Let me see · · ·
Have a think. Now, what can it be · · ?

Little Jack Horner

Little Jack Horner
sat in a corner
eating a Christmas pie.
He put in his thumb
and pulled out a plum,
and said, "What a good boy am I!"

Chop, Chop, Chop

Three tiny pairs of dark glasses
(dropped).
Three little grey tails
(cropped).

What's the answer? Let me see . . .
Have a think. Now, what can it be . . ?

Three Blind Mice

Three blind mice, three blind mice,
see how they run, see how they run.
They all ran after the farmer's wife,
who cut off their tails with a carving knife.
Did you ever see such a thing in your life
as three blind mice?

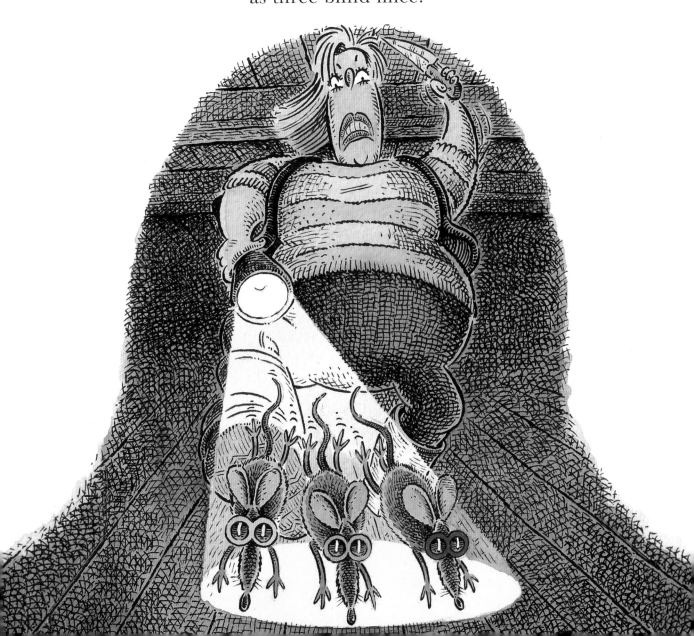

Yolk Bloke

The shell
of a great big egg
that fell
and broke,
and a suit of funny clothes
(they're covered in yolk!)

What's the answer? Let me see · · ·
Have a think. Now, what can it be · · ·?

Humpty Dumpty

Humpty Dumpty sat on a wall.
Humpty Dumpty had a great fall.
All the king's horses and all the king's men
couldn't put Humpty
together again.

Smoke Bloke

Three worn-out fiddles,
played a lot –
in fact, still hot.
A pipe (for tobacco, I think),
and a golden bowl
for drink.

What's the answer? Let me see · · ·
Have a think. Now, what can it be · · · ?

Old King Cole

Old King Cole was a merry old soul,
and a merry old soul was he.
He called for his pipe and he called for his bowl
and he called for his fiddlers three.

Every fiddler had a fine fiddle
and a very fine fiddle had he.
Oh, there's none so rare as can compare
with King Cole and his fiddlers three.

Tobacco Pouch Pooch

An empty cupboard,
completely bare,
and a dog just sitting,
waiting there,
smoking a pipe
in his owner's chair.

What's the answer? Let me see · · ·
Have a think. Now, what can it be · · ?

Old Mother Hubbard

Old Mother Hubbard
went to the cupboard
to fetch her poor dog a bone.
But when she got there
the cupboard was bare.
And so the poor dog had none.

She went to the butcher's
to fetch him some tripe.
But when she came back
he was smoking a pipe.

The dame made a curtsey.
The dog made a bow.
The dame said, "Your servant."
The dog said, "Bow-wow."

Red-Handed Robbery

A plate with crumbs
and a blob of jam,
left lying on the ground,
still warm when found,
and covered with sticky finger prints –
so someone's hands
will need a rinse!

What's the answer? Let me see · · ·
Have a think. Now, what can it be · · ?

The Queen of Hearts

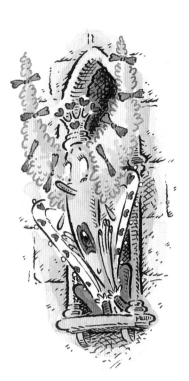

The Queen of Hearts
she made some tarts,
all on a summer's day.
The Knave of Hearts
he stole those tarts,
and took them clean away.

Supper Song

A small song-book,
put down,
a dish of butter
and a loaf of bread
(brown).

What's the answer? Let me see · · ·
Have a think. Now, what can it be · · ?

Little Tommy Tucker

Little Tommy Tucker
sings for his supper.
What shall we give him?
Brown bread and butter.

Peepo! Sheep-Ho!

A flock of sheep,
and they're on the roam.
Maybe they'll find
their own way home…?

What's the answer? Let me see · · ·
Have a think. Now, what can it be · · ?

Little Bo-Peep

Little Bo-Peep has lost her sheep
and doesn't know where to find them.
Leave them alone, and they will come home,
bringing their tails behind them.

Beep-Beep! Boy Asleep!

Here by a haystack,
not far from the corn,
someone's been sleeping –
they've dropped their horn.

What's the answer? Let me see · · ·
Have a think. Now, what can it be · · ?

Little Boy Blue

Little Boy Blue,
come blow your horn.
The sheep's in the meadow,
the cow's in the corn.

Where is the boy
who looks after the sheep?
He's under a haycock
fast asleep.

You've reached the end now.
Good. Well done.
I hope you've had some riddledy fun.
And if you didn't guess each rhyme,
well, try again another time!